KATE BENDER

THE KANSAS MURDERESS

The Horrible History of an Arch Killer

Allison Hardy

Copyright, 1944
by E. Haldeman-Julius

HALDEMAN-JULIUS PUBLICATIONS
GIRARD, KANSAS
Printed in the United States of America

KATE BENDER, THE KANSAS MURDERESS

The State of Kansas, in the 1870's, was a wild and lawless region. Like the Indian Territory which adjoined it on the South, Kansas was a haven for criminals and outlaws who had fled from more thickly populated regions in the North and East. Settlements were few and far between, and the citizens were reared in the tradition that a man's past was his own business. Such law and order as existed was administered by a few local officers, and some of these marshals were themselves fugitives from justice. This was the setting for the Bender "murder farm," where more than a score of travelers were butchered for their money. The disclosure of these crimes, in 1873, made front-page news all over the United States.

The origin of the Bender family is shrouded in mystery, and a great deal of material that has been written about them is based upon fireside tradition rather than upon established fact. One story is that they came from a German settlement in Pennsylvania, having been driven out by their neighbors because Mrs. Bender and her daughter Kate were suspected of *hexerei* or witchcraft. According to this yarn the two women went into a graveyard at midnight, in the dark of the moon, and removed every stitch of their clothing, which they hung on an infidel's tombstone. They began in German with a verbal renunciation of the Christian religion, and swore to give themselves body and soul to the devil. Then they both delivered their bodies up to the "Dark Stranger"—a man who was inducting them into the mystery. The sexual act completed, all three chanted certain obscene couplets—terrible words which assemble devils, and the spirits of the evil dead—and ended by reciting the Lord's prayer backward. This done, the two women were pronounced witches, bound by unspeakable oaths to serve their new master through all eternity.

It is a fact that many Pennsylvania Germans, even today, are firm believers in witchcraft and the like. I have myself met people in rural Pennsylvania who believe that a woman who has sold her soul to Satan in this fashion has supernatural powers, and is able to do many things which are impossible for ordinary mortals. A witch, these backwoods Germans say, can assume the form of any bird or animal, but cats and wolves seem to be her favorite disguises. Witches are supposed to delight in casting spells upon their neighbors, evil spells which cause illness or insanity or violent death. Crop failures, loss of livestock, fires, cyclones, floods and other calamities are often attributed to some woman in the neighborhood who is supposed to have sold herself to the Devil. The testimony given in court, in connection with several so-called "hex murders" in Pennsylvania only a few years ago, might have been copied from some medieval book on demonology.

The Benders were German all right, and other Germans who talked with them in Kansas said that they spoke the broken dialect of the Pennsylvania "Dutch," but the story about Kate and her mother dancing naked in the graveyard may well be apocryphal. "Though I wouldn't put it past them," as an old woman who knew the family expressed it. The early settlers in Kansas were credulous and superstitious about some things, but as a class they were not inclined to believe much in

Printing Statement:

Due to the very old age and scarcity of this book, many of the pages may be hard to read due to the blurring of the original text, possible missing pages, missing text and other issues beyond our control.

Because this is such an important and rare work, we believe it is best to reproduce this book regardless of its original condition.

Thank you for your understanding.

witchcraft. The fact that such stories were circulated at all shows that there was something peculiar about the Bender family.

When the Benders came to Labette county, Kansas, in 1870, there were four persons in the family group. John Bender, the head of the family, was apparently about 60 years of age. He was a short, stocky fellow with a ruddy complexion. His sandy hair was rather long, and he wore a full beard and mustache in the fashion of the time. He had a sullen expression, and "never looked a feller in the eye," as one of his associates remarked. He talked little, at least when strangers were about, and spoke only German. It is said that he could understand English, but there is no record that he ever spoke a word of it, except for two or three vulgar expletives.

John Bender's wife was short of stature, and rather stout. She had blue eyes and brown hair, and seemed to be about 10 years younger than her husband. She spoke broken English as well as German, but was not talkative. In the records that I have seen, she is always referred to as Mrs. John Bender—it appears that none of the neighbors ever called her anything else. It seems very odd that the persons who claimed to have been intimately associated with the Benders did not know the old woman's Christian name..

Young Johnny Bender was a slim, rather handsome chap about 25 years old. He had brown hair and blue eyes, and spoke English fluently but with a strong German accent. Young Johnny was more inclined to sociability than either of the elder Benders.

A much more striking personality was Kate Bender, the only daughter of the house. She was tall, slender, good-looking, probably not more than 20 years of age. She had a strong face "like a young eagle," with flashing dark eyes. Her hair was black, but many persons remarked that it had a reddish cast in the sunlight. Kate spoke good English with little accent, and was affable and glib in talking with any stranger who took her fancy.

It was generally believed that John Bender was not the father of Johnny or Kate. The story is that Johnny and Kate were the children of Mrs. Bender by a former marriage to a man named Gebhardt, but they both used the name Bender in Kansas. Some newspaper writers have asserted that the two were not brother and sister at all—that Johnny was Kate's lover who had followed the Benders from Pennsylvania. Others have said that Johnny and Kate were brother and sister all right, but that they lived together in an incestuous relationship. I have no evidence that there is any truth in this latter view, although incest was not uncommon on the border in pioneer days.

When the Benders first came to Kansas they lived on a farm somewhere near Parsons, in a rather isolated spot. Dr. George W. Gabriel, of Parsons, remembered them well. "The first time I recall meeting any of the Benders," he wrote, "was in the fall of 1871 at the home of a sick family named Boyd. The old woman and Kate were there. The Benders were German and talked the language considerably. When outsiders were present they often carried on a conversation among themselves in their native tongue. Kate talked glibly in English also, and was *active in what she termed spiritualism.*" Dr. Gabriel does not say so, but he knew what Kate and the old woman were doing at the Boyd home. They were accustomed to visit the sick all over the neighborhood, and claimed to cure diseases by some supernatural hokuspokus.

It must have been late in 1871 when the Benders left the farm, and moved to a place on the Parsons road, about seven miles northeast of Cherryvale. This was the main road, much used by travelers between Fort Scott and Independence, Kansas, and on southeast into the Indian Territory. The Bender cabin had only one room, but as they saw so many prosperous looking strangers on the road, the family decided to go into the hotel business. They divided the house into two rooms by hanging a heavy canvas curtain across the middle of the building. In the front room they put a small stock of groceries, canned goods, preserved fruits, tobacco and the like. The rear room was a combined kitchen and dining-room, and there Mrs. Bender and Kate served meals to hungry wayfarers. There were no proper beds, but the family slept on pallets made up on the floor. Travelers usually had their own bedding, and were content to camp in the yard when the weather was fine. In case of a sudden storm they brought their blankets into the house and bedded down on the floor with the Benders.

The food and lodging offered at the Bender Tavern wasn't anything to write home about, but it was better than sleeping out on the prairie and cooking one's own grub. There was a rude barn not far from the house, where the traveler's horses were fed and attended to, this being young Johnny's specialty. There were many such places on the Kansas prairies in those days, when everybody travelled on horseback or in wagons.

"Here in this roadside inn," says an anonymous writer in the Kansas City *Journal*, "a seeming haven to weary travelers, the Benders systematically carried on the business of murder and robbery. How soon after arriving in the country they began their bloody work, or who was their first victim or how many they killed, is not known. From the fact that numerous missing travelers were never accounted for, their fate being a mystery to this day, it is reasonable and logical to suppose the toll of life taken was considerable, and that there were a large number of undiscovered dead."

We do know, however, that the Benders went about the business of wholesale murder with a typical German thoroughness. The Bender Tavern was less than a hundred yards from the main road, set out on the open prairie without so much as a large tree to shelter it from the public gaze. Obviously it was not practicable to carry dead men out of the house in the daytime, so the Benders devised a hiding-place for corpses inside the building. They dug a pit under the kitchen, and hinged a concealed trapdoor in the rough floor. The Benders did not care for farming, but they planted some seedling apples and peach trees out behind the tavern, and the ground in this orchard was always freshly plowed. A little stream called Drum Creek meandered over the prairie not far from the orchard, and Big Hill Creek was only three miles away.

In the Winter of 1872 the body of a man was found in Big Hill Creek, about four miles from the Tavern, but nobody was able to identify him. A doctor who examined the corpse said that the poor fellow had been murdered—knocked on the head with some instrument like a hammer, and stabbed about the throat with a big knife. Crimes of violence were not uncommon in Kansas, and this victim was a stranger anyhow, so the boys just buried him out on the prairie and said no more about it. Nobody thought of connecting Kate Bender with the crime. The Benders were regarded as rather peculiar people, not very neighborly, but had never been involved in any local scandals, and nobody ever dreamed that the "Dutch folks" were cold-blooded murderers.

A month or so later another body was found, floating in the Verdigris River not far from Cherryvale. This time some local people were aroused, and tried to identify the corpse as one of the men who had been reported missing recently. A regular inquest was held, and a sort of indignation meeting took place in an old building in Cherryvale. It may be that John Bender attended this meeting as several newspaper writers have said, although it does not seem likely. An account in a popular magazine would have us to believe that "John Bender was among the loudest in denouncing the crime and demanding that the killer be apprehended," but this is surely an error, since John Bender did not speak English.

Old Mrs. Bender still visited the sick, and worked charms and healing witchcraft occasionally, but Kate resolved to make a regular business of this sort of thing. Several of her professional cards, and a printed handbill which she scattered about southeastern Kansas, are still in existence. The handbill reads as follows:

Prof. Miss KATIE BENDER

Can heal all sorts of Diseases; can cure Blindness, Fits, Deafness and all such Diseases, also Deaf and Dumbness.

Residence 14 miles East of Independence, on the road from Independence to Osage Mission, one and one-half miles East of Norahead Station.

KATIE BENDER

June 18, 1872.

Not so many years ago there were people in Kansas who believed that Kate Bender really had supernatural powers of one kind or another. They said that she not only cured diseases, but located lost articles, understood astrology and numerology, read palms, told fortunes by means of sticks-and-buttons, worked spells against evil women, and sold infallible luck charms and love-potions.

One story widely circulated was that the Benders had no milk-cows, but always served plenty of milk, butter and homemade cheese. Since they did not leave the Tavern for weeks at a time, people could not understand where these dairy products were coming from. Finally a wandering cowpuncher peeked in at the window, hoping to see the shapely Kate in the act of undressing. Instead he saw Kate and the old woman hang some dishrags on a wire in front of the kitchen stove, and squeeze several gallons of milk out of the rags! A farmer 10 miles off said that his cows were being milked without his knowledge or consent, and that on one occasion he had actually seen the udders of two cows diminish in size, as if they were being milked, although nobody was within reach of them.

One of the charms against witches and evil spirits generally, which it is said that Kate Bender imparted to her clients for the sum of 50c, is written down in an autograph album dated 1873:

Dullix, ix, ux,
You can't come over Pontio
Pontio is above Pilato!

All one had to do, according to the old belief, was to cross the first two fingers of each hand and recite these words in time of peril.

Another fantastic tale about Kate Bender is that she was accustomed to visit a certain farmer who lived about two miles distant, in the guise of a house-cat. Once inside his shanty, she would resume her normal shape and spend the night with him. When she wanted to leave his place she became a cat again, returned to the Bender house, and was transformed into a woman before any other member of the family realized that Kate had been absent..

A family named Weissbrod, who came to Kansas from central Missouri, promulgated the theory that a witch could always be detected by fixing a sharp nail in the seat of her chair, so that about half-an-inch of the point protrudes. Then one has only to get the suspected witch to sit down in the chair. If she is really a witch she will not feel the point at all, so that if a woman jumps up and cries out it means that she is innocent. The story goes that one of the boys tried this on Kate Bender, and succeeded in getting her to sit on a piece of pointed wire. She sprang up immediately, knocked the young man down, and kicked him several times with her heavy boots before he could get away. "She hollered so loud you could hear her 10 miles off," the boy reported later. "She ain't no witch, but if there's any more testin' to be done, you'll have to git somebody else to 'tend to it."

The Weissbrods introduced several other notions about the best methods of protection against witchcraft—evidently old German folklore similar to that which the Benders themselves had brought from Pennsylvania. One highly recommended procedure was to drive three nails in the door, in the form of a triangle to represent the Father, Son and Holy Ghost. Another was to paint the outside of the door blue—this was said to keep the goblins out of the household. Some Kansans nailed a horse-shoe up above the door, as a sort of general prophylatic against witches, bad luck in cooking, venereal diseases and other forms of evil. Other pioneers nailed up two little sticks in the shape of a cross, believing that this was more efficacious than the horse-shoe. There is no doubt that all of these things were done in southeastern Kansas in the early 70's, but it is by no means certain that they were directed especially against Kate Bender. A few people evidently regarded Kate as a witch, and it may be that some suspected the Benders of murdering their guests, but if so they said little about it at the time. After the great exposure in 1873, many persons popped up claiming that they had tried to warn travelers against the bloody Benders, but that nobody would listen to their warnings.

It is odd how many travelers came forward after the crimes had been discovered, with strange tales of their own narrow escapes from death at the hands of the Bender family. One of these was a Catholic priest, Father Paul Ponziglione, whose story was told in a local newspaper. "On a windy day toward dusk, Father Paul arrived at the Bender place and decided to put up there for the night. His suspicions were aroused when he happened to see the old man Bender place a heavy hammer on the other side of the curtain, just back of the supper table. Later he observed the old man and Kate holding a low, whispered conversation. The hard and forbidding features of the Benders, the lonely surroundings, and the moaning of the wind had a far from soothing effect on the priest's mind. He remembered reading about the strange disappearance of persons in that part of the state, of whom no trace had ever been found. The more he studied over the matter, the more uneasy he became. Some warning voice within seemed to urge his immediate departure. Finally, under pretext of looking after his horses, he left the house, hurriedly hitched his team to the spring wagon and drove rapidly away. Long afterward Father Paul often told the story of his escape from the terrible Benders, and he always added that he owed his safe deliverance to a Higher Power."

Father Ponziglione's story is straightforward and has a ring of truth about it, but I have found no evidence that he ever told anybody of his experience until after the Bender's criminal activities were exposed to all the world. Some of Father Paul's imitators told much wilder and more fantastic tales, like that of the schoolmaster from Paola, Kansas. This man said that he rode up to the Bender Tavern at dusk and was about ready to dismount, when suddenly he saw in the evening sky a gigantic skull and cross-bones, "exactly like the sign on poison bottles in the drug-store!" This apparation so alarmed him that he spurred his horse back to the main road and fled toward Independence at a full gallop, with never a pause until the animal was completely exhausted.

Another story is told of a young couple who came along in a wagon with their feeble-minded child, a boy about 10 years old who had never spoken an intelligible word. The husband pulled up his team to turn into the Bender place, when suddenly the boy rose up from the bed of the wagon, where he lay on a pile of hay covered with an old quilt. Showing every symptom of fear and horror, the idiot shrieked "Blood! Blood!" and made as if to climb out of the wagon. The astounded parents soothed the child and drove on, having decided to camp by the roadside instead of lodging at the Bender place. As someone pointed out at the time, neither the schoolmaster nor the parents of the idiot child were in any real danger. The Benders murdered only for the purpose of robbery, and shabby folk with poor horses and no money were safe enough at the Bender Tavern.

After the exposure of the Benders in 1873, many other strange stories came to light. One traveler testified that he had approached the Tavern one stormy night and rapped on the door without getting any response, although he could hear music and human voices inside. Finally he pushed open the door and entered to find the little building jammed with strangers, who stood about playing guitars and "funny flutes." In a little space in the center of the room Kate Bender and another girl were dancing, naked except for some flashy jewelry "which seemed to have feathers fastened to it." The spectators were all dark, black-eyed people, wearing outlandish gaudy clothes and speaking a foreign tongue. The traveler could not understand a word of the talk that he heard that night, and could tell nothing about the language except that it was neither English nor German. He said that it "might be some kind of Injun talk," although the people were not like any Indians he had ever seen. Later a lawyer showed this man some pictures of the Seminole Indians from Florida, and he thought that the company at Benders' Tavern might have been Seminoles. Some local officers who laughed at the idea of a Seminole invasion of Kansas believed that the Benders' guests were gypsies, since some of these strange people had been seen near Fort Scott a month or so before. The officers were inclined to link this traveler's tale up with a theory that Mrs. Bender and Kate were not Pennsylvania Germans at all, but Gypsies who had lived in some German-speaking part of Central Europe. It fits in well with the view that the Benders were associated with a band of criminals who helped them dispose of the valuables taken from their victims, and explains in a measure the strange events which transpired after their crimes were discovered.

Some newspaper writers have repeated the story of William Pickering, who said that he once stopped at the Bender Tavern for dinner. A young woman, who must have been Kate Bender, engaged him in a provocative conversation for some time, and finally invited him to sit at the table with his back against a heavy canvas curtain. About to do so, Pickering noticed dark stains on the curtain, about the height of a seated man's head. He didn't like to sit with his head and the back of his fancy shirt so near this dirty cloth, so he sat down on the other side of the table, facing the curtain instead of leaning back against it. This seemed to upset both of the elder Benders, who scowled at him and exchanged a few words in German, which Pickering did not understand. "That's Paw's place," said Kate sharply. Pickering stood up then, and both he and Kate spoke loudly and angrily. Pickering finally shouted that there was only one clean place in the house, and if he could not sit there he would not eat in the damned shack at all. Kate snatched up a kitchen-knife and rushed at Pickering, who fled from the house, followed by a stream of invective from Kate. Young Pickering mounted his horse and rode away. He was angry, but not at all frightened, as he did not realize the danger. He thought that the Benders were simply bad-tempered foreigners who kept a filthy tavern. He had no idea that they were a gang of murderers, who had planned to kill him for the sake of some gold coins he had shown to Kate while the old woman was preparing dinner.

An elderly couple named Gould, who lived in Girard, Kansas, in the 90's, used to tell some extraordinary stories about the Benders. As I understand it, the Goulds had never seen any member of the Bender family, but got their information from some of the neighbors, a group of people who were interested in spiritualism, table-tipping, automatic writing, astrology, mental healing, witchcraft and occult matters generally. When the Goulds joined this little band of amateur psychic researchers, they found that several of their new friends had visited Kate Bender in 1872 and thought highly of her mediumistic and other supernatural powers. One woman who lived on a farm between Girard and Fort Scott had lost two valuable rings under mysterious conditions. She was alone in the house when the rings disappeared, and it seemed impossible for anybody to have stolen them. Still, the rings were missing, and a search of the whole place failed to reveal their whereabouts.

When the woman drove to the Bender Tavern, Kate talked with her for a while, and then went into a sort of trance. In this condition she said that both rings would be found in the wooden gutter attached to the roof of the house. When the woman got back home she was rather ashamed of having made the trip, and regarded the $5 fee that she had paid Kate Bender as wasted. But she got a ladder and climbed upon the roof, and found one of the rings just where Kate had said it was! She told her husband about the whole adventure, and he mounted the ladder and searched carefully, but did not locate the second ring. Late that night it occurred to him that it might be well to look in the rain-barrel. So the two got out of bed, lighted a latern, and went out into the yard. The water in the rain-barrel was dark with soot, but when they dipped the water out, the woman found her ring in the silt at the bottom of the barrel. It had been in the gutter, evidently, and had been washed down into the barrel by a recent rain!

This story of the recovered rings is doubtless a lie, but the Goulds heard it and believed it, as did their little circle of occult-minded friends. It is worth reporting here as an example of the stories that were circulated at the time, and goes far to explain the superstitious awe with which some people regarded the alleged powers of "Prof. Miss Kate Bender."

Since Kate was so successful in finding lost jewelry and locating strayed or stolen livestock, it was natural that people should call on her for information about their missing friends and relatives. It was surprising, when one stopped to think about it, how many men "showed up missin'" in that sparsely settled section of southeastern Kansas. These mysterious disappearances were noted in the newspapers, but Kate Bender and other local miracle-workers were unable to solve any of them. There was no evidence of crime in these cases. The fact that Kate was so often consulted indicates that nobody, at this time, suspected the Bender family of any connection with the missing persons, beyond the fact that some of them were known to have stopped at the Tavern for a meal or a night's rest.

Kate told most of the persons who consulted her professionally that the missing men were alive and well, on their way to the Indian Territory, or Texas, or some other not-too-distant region. She wept as she assured one poor woman that her vanished husband had eloped with an Indian girl into what is now Oklahoma, and that she would never see his face again! Despite Kate's brilliant success in other fields, there is no record that she ever located a single one of the travelers who had disappeared in Labette county between 1870 and 1873. It was not lack of knowledge that caused her failure, however. The truth is that Kate and her family had murdered at least a score of these pilgrims, and that many of them were buried in the Bender orchard, only a few yards distant from the building in which Kate was talking with their distressed relatives.

In nearly every case, men who traveled in company, or who arrived at the Tavern when other guests were present, were perfectly safe at the Benders' place. Kate was the brains of the outfit, and she did not believe in taking chances. She realized that no man, be he ever so effective a fighter, was a match for four persons who caught him unawares. But if the Benders should attack a party of two or three men at one time, there was always the danger that one of the travelers might escape. And one escape, of course, would ruin the Benders forever. It is interesting to speculate upon what would have happened if Wild Bill Hickok, who was not many miles distant at the time, should have chanced to drop in at the Bender place. Hickok was always alert, and given the slightest suspicion that something was amiss, he might have killed all four Benders in something less than three seconds. The probability is, however, that Kate would have pulled the wool over his eyes somehow, and the great gun-fighter would have been buried in the orchard along with the rest of the boys.

When the Benders were alone at the Tavern, and a solitary rider was seen approaching, there was much hurrying to and fro. Kate hastened to put on a crisp house-dress, calculated to emphasize her best points. The old woman stirred up a fire in the cookstove, and contrived to warm up something that would at least give off an appetizing odor. Young Johnny and old man Bender made their preparations also, as will appear later.

The Benders' method was simple enough. The first job was to find out whether or not a guest had money on his person, or hidden about his wagon or other equipment. It seems that Johnny always took care of the horses, and while he was feeding the animal he looked for concealed saddle-pockets or other common frontier devices for carrying money. It was customary for travelers to carry considerable amounts of cash in those days, since banks were few and far between. Even a shabby-looking rider might have several hundred dollars on his person, but there was also a big revolver or a concealed Derringer to protect his wealth. Some men carried money loose in their pockets, or in a wallet, but most experienced travelers preferred a money-belt of soft-tanned leather, worn around the waist under the clothing. Kate was a good-looking woman, although not such a devastating beauty as the imaginative reporters made her appear. But she could behave very provocatively on occasion, and a little playful scuffling usually enabled her to find out whether a man was wearing a money-belt, and whether it was fat or lean. If it were lean, the man was allowed to leave the place unharmed; but if the belt was fat with greenbacks, the poor fellow's doom was sealed.

If it seemed practicable, the Benders waited until nightfall, and then the unsuspecting guest was lured out into the darkness on some pretext or other. If he was an old man, or a man interested in food or sleep rather than in sex, Johnny and the old man attended to this part of the business. If the fellow was amorously inclined, it was Kate who arranged to meet him in the shrubbery behind the house. In either case, one of the Bender men struck the poor fellow on the head with a heavy hammer. This should have been enough to kill an ordinary man, but the Benders took no chances. Immediately after the blow was struck, Kate was on the victim like a wildcat, with a razor-edged kitchen knife in her hand. Generally she just cut his throat from ear to ear, but in several cases she stabbed him in the breast for good measure. Men who examined the bodies of the victims said that in one instance the corpse had been disemboweled and the sex organs mutilated. The explanations which have been offered for this mutilation have to do with the practice of witchcraft, but they seem so ridiculous that I cannot bring myself to set them down in this book.

When the traveler was dead the Benders lost no time in removing his valuables, then Johnny and the old man carried the body out to the orchard. Usually a shallow grave had been prepared in advance, and covered with an old barn door, which in turn was hidden by a thin sprinkling of dirt. Lifting this rude cover, they pitched the body into the hole and filled the grave as best they could. Next morning the two men were out at dawn, leveling the whole thing off and carefully removing any blood that might have been spilled unseen in the darkness. The neighbors had often remarked the frequency with which the little orchard was plowed the year around, but this was regarded as "a fool Dutch notion"—it never occurred to anybody to connect it with secret burials.

If for any reason the Benders thought best to murder a man in the daylight hours, they knocked him off inside the house. Sometimes it seems that Kate threw her arms around him, or pretended to be reading his palm, while Johnny slipped up behind the poor chap and smashed his skull with the hammer. If anything went wrong, Kate herself was in a position to stab him before he could do any damage to the Benders. Sometimes they seated the traveler at the table with his back to the curtain separating the two rooms of the Tavern. With the light from the big window in front, the victim's position was easily seen through the curtain. All that Johnny or the old man had to do was wait, until the fellow leaned back so his head touched the curtain. Then a heavy blow of the hammer, right through the canvas, did the business. Kate sprang forward and cut the man's throat almost before the body touched the floor. A few seconds later the corpse was thrown down into a pit under the kitchen, and the trapdoor closed. It required only a moment for Kate and the old woman to wipe up any blood that had been spilled. Another wayfarer who entered the place three minutes after the fatal blow was struck would see nothing out of the ordinary—certainly no evidence of a bloody murder.

A body in the pit under the secret trapdoor was left there until after dark, when the Benders searched it for valuables and then carried it out to be buried with the others in the orchard. Nobody has ever been able to figure out just what disposal was made of the horses, wagons, saddles, harness and so on which must have been left at the Bender stable. Several of the horses and wagons belonging to men murdered at the Bender place were of distinctive appearance, and would have been recognized instantly by scores of people along the roads in southeastern Kansas. Not one of these horses, nor a single piece of equipment, was ever seen after the owner's disappearance, so far as I have been able to find out. It was in fact this, more than anything else, which convinced many persons that the Benders were associated with a band of Gypsies, or perhaps a gang of Indian horse-thieves, who somehow spirited this booty away down into Oklahoma and Texas, where it could be sold to strangers. Some officers thought that the Benders must have killed the horses and concealed the carcasses somehow, and probably destroyed the expensive buggies and saddles, too. But nobody who knew the Bender family believed for a moment that they could ever bring themselves to destroy anything that could be sold for considerable sums of money. "There ain't a Dutchman in the wolrd could have done it," one old man assured reporters. "I know the Dutch from away back, and they just ain't built that way." And it is a fact that the Benders always lived very frugally, apparently regarding the accumulation of money as the most important thing in the world.

They must have been pretty successful in their efforts to obtain wealth: Two of the men who had disappeared in the neighborhood, Ben Brown and W. F. McCarthy, were known to have carried $1,500 and $3,000 each, besides some valuable jewelry and other trinkets. A man named McCugsey, who disappeared about the same time, was believed to have had at least $2,000 on his person. And there were several others, including a woman who had several valuable antique diamond rings. Add to this the small but steady sale of food and accomodations at the Tavern, and the fairly good income which "Prof. Miss Kate Bender" derived from her supernatural healing and other occult practices, and it is plain that the Bender family must have done very well financially. If Kate had been smart enough to spare Dr. William York, a prominent physician of Independence, Kansas, the Benders could probably have continued to ply their bloody trade for many years without much danger of detection.

The story goes that Dr. York had been visiting his brother, Colonel A. M. York, in Fort Scott, Kansas. It was on March 9, 1873, that he started back to his home in Independence. He rode a fine saddle-mare, carried an expensive watch, and had between $700 and $900 in his wallet. He spent the first night at the Osage Mission, which he left the morning of March 10. Meeting some friends on the road, he remarked that he expected to eat dinner at the Bender Tavern. That was the last time Dr. York was seen alive. When he failed to arrive at Independence his friends showed some concern, but it seems not to have occurred to any of them that he had met with foul play. Life was a leisurely affair in Kansas in those days, and it was not unlikely that the doctor had ridden over to some other settlement to spend a few days with friends..

A Kansas City newspaper account of the Bender affair contains the following: "At the Spring election, the second Tuesday in April, 1873, which was held in a schoolhouse about two miles from the Bender place, a number of men gathered in the building, as it was a bad day. Among them was John Bender, curled up on a bench, apparently asleep. Among the topics of conversation, was the number of persons who had been reported missing lately. Several of them had been traced to that neighborhood, and then the trail was lost. Among those mentioned was Dr. York, who was locally well known and who at one time had been a member of the legislature. The remark was made that some suspected that the missing man had been murdered in that vicinity. Whereupon one man spoke up: 'If that is found to be true, I will help burn the guilty parties at the stake!' The other men present agreed that they would help, too." During this talk old man Bender lay on his bench, apparently asleep. But the reporter adds that he might have understood the talk that was going on around him, and that the threat of lynch law may have influenced his actions later on.

The other persons who had disappeared in the neighborhood doubtless caused some talk at the time, and some slight effort was made to trace them, but nothing ever really came of the matter. They were strangers traveling through the country, or local men of no great importance, and their deaths had not aroused any intensive investigation. But the Dr. York case was something else again. Dr. York himself was a widely known and popular man, and his brother was one of the big shots of southeastern Kansas. When Dr. York did not show up for nearly six weeks, and nothing was heard from him, the Colonel organized a search party and went over the whole route between Independence and the place near Osage Mission where the doctor had met his friends on the road.

Colonel York and his men took plenty of time. They stopped at every house within two or three miles of the road, and asked the farmers whether they had seen a man answering to Dr. York's description, or a horse which resembled his. They described the doctor's saddle, and his watch, and his revolver, and his wallet. They found many people along the road toward Fort Scott who had seen the missing man pass, but nobody south or west of the Bender place knew anything about him.

On April 24, accompanied by 12 friends from the vicinity of Cherryvale, Colonel York rode up to the Bender Tavern. Old John Bender and young Johnny met them in the yard, and Johnny answered all their questions. Old man Bender, who was reading a German Bible as the posse rode up, tried to answer also, but nobody could understand him, so he spoke in German and young Johnny translated both questions and answers. Both men said that Dr. York had come to the Tavern about noon, eaten his dinner, and left shortly after one o'clock. He had talked little, and said nothing about where he was going, but the Benders had assumed that he was on his way to Independence, since they knew that he resided there.

Somebody had seen some strangers camping near Drum Creek, not far from the Bender home, and Johnny Bender suggested that they might have had something to do with the doctor's disappearance. The posse found the remains of a campfire on the bank of a creek, but no evidence that Dr. York had ever been at camp. It happened that there was a deep hole in the creek-bed just at this point, so several of the men dragged the creek on the chance that the missing doctor's body might be concealed beneath the muddy water. Young Johnny Bender helped in this work, but found nothing.

After dragging the creek, the posse returned to the Bender Tavern, and Colonel York insisted upon seeing Kate Bender, of whom he had heard so much. Old man Bender did not like this, but the armed posse brushed aside his protests and walked into the house. Old Mrs. Bender was lying on a cot, and said that she was not feeling well. Kate was sprightly as usual, and declared herself willing to answer any questions. Colonel York said politely that he had heard much of her clairvoyant powers, and that since all ordinary investigations had failed to locate his brother, he had come to consult her professionally. "My brother William has been missing for six weeks," he said. "I fear for his safety. But I will gladly pay you $500 if your supernatural power can reveal to me his present whereabouts, whether he is alive or dead."

Kate answered him by repeating the story told previously by young Johnny, corroborating his evidence in every detail, and adding that she remembered Dr. York very well, since she had waited upon him herself. "As to my clairvoyance," she added, "you have heard aright. I have, at times, the power to locate lost objects and missing persons. But I cannot do this on such short notice— I must have time to prepare myself for the trance, to work myself up into proper state of mind. Even then, I do not always succeed. But in this case I shall do my best, whether you see fit to pay me $500 or not. If you will return in two or three days, I shall doubtless have some information for you about your brother's fate."

According to some accounts of the affair, a member of the posse found a gold tie-pin in the dust near the house, which Colonel York identified as having belonged to his brother. The colonel naturally became suspicious, but Kate assured him that she had never seen the pin before, and that if it belonged to Dr. York he had evidently dropped it near the spot where his horse was tied. This story of the pin has been often reprinted, and one famous illustrated magazine years later printed a photograph of the stick-pin. But the whole account of this incident may have been a fabrication. Several members of the posse when interviewed later had not seen any such pin, or heard anything of its being found. Since they were all present at the house, it is strange that they should have failed to see the pin, or to hear the conversation which Colonel York was alleged to have had with Kate Bender about it. Several of these men told reporters that they all rode away from the Benders' place that day fully convinced that the Benders had told the truth, and that Dr. York must have met disaster at some undetermined point between the Bender Tavern and Independence. Several of them believed that Kate's supernatural powers might reveal vital information about the doctor's disappearance, but most of them thought that her clairvoyance was a fake. Colonel York himself was inclined to be skeptical. "However," he said, "if she can tell me where my brother is, or locate his body for me, I shall be glad to pay her $500. And if she fails to find him, there's no harm done, and I won't pay a red cent!"

I have found no record of Colonel York returning to the Bender Tavern in two or three days, as Kate had suggested. About a week after the posse's interview with Kate, two neighbors passing the Bender place heard a hungry calf bawling in its pen, and the noise of a cow trying to reach it. That same day Silas Toles and his brother Pete, who lived not far off, came over to the Tavern but found it deserted. They turned the cow and calf out, and then went into the building. Everything was in great disorder, as if the Benders had left in a hurry. Dirty dishes and fragments of cooked food were scattered all over the place. Pictures were pulled down off the walls, and the curtain which had separated the two rooms was lying bundled up in a corner. The stove was full of light ashes, as if a lot of papers had been burned. The big Bible which old man Bender had read so ostentatiously had been flung down behind the table. The Toles brothers looked the situation over, but they did not find anything interesting. They did not find the secret trapdoor leading to the pit under the kitchen, for instance. They told the neighbors that the Benders had rushed off somewhere in a hurry, and that was all that anybody knew about it.

About this time, or perhaps a few days earlier, a man who lived near Thayer, Kansas, found a team and wagon in a densely wooded valley. The horses were unhitched but tied to the wagon with rope halters. They had evidently been there for some days, as they had eaten every blade of grass and every leaf that they could reach, and were thin. There was a cur dog in the wagon, and it was nearly starved. Also in the wagon was an old shotgun which had been fired, the bed of the wagon being full of holes. There was no blood, or any other sign that anyone had been hurt there. Nobody in the neighborhood of Thayer could identify this outfit, so they took it to town and left the whole thing at the livery-stable. Later on some people who had lived near the Benders said that the team and wagon belonged to young Johnny Bender.

News traveled rather slowly on the Kansas border in those days, and the Benders had been gone about two weeks before Colonel York was notified. As soon as he heard of this development he came down from Fort Scott with several friends, and made a painstaking examination of the Bender property. It was Colonel York himself, according to the chroniclers, who found the carefully hidden trapdoor in the kitchen. He went down into the pit himself, with a latern, and noted a disagreeable odor. There were no bodies in the pit, but the dirt floor of the place had been soaked with blood. A large crowd of people from nearby settlements had collected by this time, and many of them believed that the bodies of murdered men must be somehow concealed under the house. The building rested almost on the ground, and it was difficult for a man to get under the floor, except at the place where the pit was located. So the assembled farmers placed logs under the building to serve as rollers, and then hitched their teams to the Tavern itself. By this means they soon rolled the building away from its original position, so that the earth underneath was open to inspection.

A careful search of the ground which had been under the Tavern showed nothing of any significance, beyond the fact that the bottom of the pit was soaked with blood. Inside the house were three heavy hammers, and one of these seemed to have traces of blood upon it. A sharp knife was found inside an old clock, and some members of the posse thought there were faint blood-stains upon the wooden handle. In the same old clock were found several cheap cuff-links and other trinkets. Some of these odds-and-ends were later found to have been the property of one of the missing men, but this was not known at the time. Except for the blood in the pit under the kitchen, nothing had been discovered which definitely linked the Benders with any crime.

There were some strange designs scratched into the floor of the front room, and Colonel York studied these for a long time. There were 12 distinct characters, arranged in a circle about three feet in diameter, with several columns of figures beside them. Finally it was decided that these devices were intended to represent the signs of the Zodiac, and had doubtless been used by Kate Bender in some of her astrological ceremonies. Half burned in the ash-heap were two little wooden figures with nails driven into them; these were probably spite-dolls, such as are still used by so-called witches in some magical hokus-pokus designed to bring disease and death upon the persons whom the dolls are supposed to represent.

After a while Colonel York, having examined everything in and under the building, took his place on the seat of a wagon in the yard. This slight elevation gave him a good view of the premises, and he gazed out moodily into the orchard which the Benders had kept so carefully plowed. Suddenly he stood up. "Boys, I see *graves* out there!" he cried excitedly. His friends did not take this seriously at first, but finally some of them climbed up on the roof of the Tavern, from which point of vantage they could study the terrain more effectively. Some of them said they too could make out several long, narrow depressions in the plowed ground between the stunted seedlings. Finally it was decided to take a slender iron rod from one of the wagons, and poke around the slight depressions in the orchard.

A few minutes of this poking about was sufficient to locate three soft spots, where it was evident that the soil had been disturbed to a considerable depth. Several men hurried away to obtain shovels and picks, and within a few minutes the body of a man came to light. This corpse was pretty badly decomposed, and it was not identified by any of those present. The man had been murdered, right enough. His throat was cut from ear to ear, and the back of his skull was crushed. The depression in the skull exactly fitted one of the blacksmith's hammers found in the Bender Tavern. There was no longer any doubt, in the minds of those present, that the Benders were a gang of murderers.

The diggers set to work furiously with pick and shovel to open the next grave, and this contained the body of Dr. York. The corpse of the missing physician was in a good state of preservation, and was recognized at once by many witnesses. The hole in the back of the head matched well with the hammer used in the other killing, and the throat was cut also. Colonel York examined the body for certain identifying marks, and then went back to the Tavern and sat down. He said that there was no doubt that the second body unearthed was that of his brother. By this time all the settlers for miles around had gathered at the Bender orchard, and Colonel York took no further part in the exhumation. There is still in existence a photograph of the scene, showing perhaps a hundred men standing about, with seven corpses lying on the ground. The picture shows several rude pine boxes beside the newly opened graves. Doubtless these boxes were used as coffins, when the bodies were loaded into wagons and hauled away to a more fitting burial-ground.

The photograph mentioned above is interesting, because photographs were not common on the frontier in the early days. It shows a large group of men, some of them wearing sombreros and rough clothing and high boots, while others were dressed in frock coats and striped trousers. Two or three wore high silk hats—the badge of the professional man. Although only seven corpses are shown in the photograph, there is no doubt that 11 were dug up in the Bender orchard. Ten of these had been struck on the head with the hammer, and had their throats cut, while two of them were otherwise mutilated by knife wounds. Nine of the victims were men, one was a young woman, and one a little girl perhaps 10 or 12 years old. The body of the girl was found beneath that of a man, later identified as her father, George Longcors of West Virginia. The little girl's body bore no wounds at all, but a piece of silk cloth was tied tightly about her throat. She was either choked or buried alive—the doctors who examined the body could not determine which.

The crowd shown in the photograph mentioned consisted entirely of men, but drawing published in Eastern newspapers and magazines depicted many women as well, wearing the "modified hoops" of the period. There can be no doubt that women and children drove out from all of the nearby towns in buggies. The newspapers of Kansas City, St. Louis and even Chicago sent reporters to the scene immediately, and they interviewed country folk all over the place. Many magazines, even *Harper's Weekly* in New York, were represented by correspondents, photographers and illustrators. Photographs in magazines were rare in those days, and most magazine pictures were pencil drawings. When a photograph was reproduced it appeared as a sort of tracing, labelled "drawn from a photograph."

All the bodies except two were ultimately identified as those of travelers, who had evidently stopped at the Bender Tavern for food and lodging. Some of the corpses were only partially clad, the most valuable items of their attire having been removed; this fact seemed to indicate that the Benders had some means of selling such stuff in distant sections of the country. This was pointed out by those who adhered to the theory that the Bender family was somehow connected with a gang, and that the Bender Tavern was only one link in a chain of "murder farms." There was good reason for believing that the 11 corpses disinterred in the orchard did not represent all of the persons murdered by the Benders. In one shallow grave the searchers found what seemed to be parts of several bodies, which had evidently been dismembered. Some of these disarticulated bones were blackened, as if an attempt had been made to destroy them by fire.

The people in southeastern Kansas were infuriated to the point of frenzy by the discovery of the Bender murders. The local newspapers printed long denunciations of the "Human Hyenas in Spiritualist Circles," "Murder Among the Astrologists," "Bloodthirsty Fortune Tellers," and the like. Harmless palmists, mental healers, fortune-tellers and crystal gazers were threatened by mobs in many parts of Kansas, and one poor fellow who called himself a "Necromancer and Psychic Clairvoyant" barely escaped with his life. A band of Gypsies, who had probably never done anything worse than cheat some farmer in a horse-trade, were beaten and robbed. Many palmists and fortune-tellers shut up shop and left the region under cover of night. Because the Benders were German there was a movement to expel all "dirty Dutchmen" from the region, but this did not get far, because there were many prosperous and respectable German farmers about, who spoke their minds in no uncertain language. But there can be no doubt that hard feelings and bitterness which arose over the Bender trouble persisted for many years—over a quarter of a century in some cases.

According to one widely accepted story of the time, in part substantiated by a printed account in the possession of the Kansas State Historical Society, Kate Bender had been involved in a love-affair with Rudolph Brockman (sometimes spelled Breckerman) who lived somewhere in the vicinity of the Bender Tavern. It is said that Brockman had courted Kate for some time, had given her considerable sums of money, had fought with young Johnny Bender on her account, and had arranged to marry her on Easter Sunday, 1873. The marriage had been postponed several times because Kate had shown Brockman some complicated astrological sharts, and explained that it would never do for them to marry until the various planets were in "the proper nuptial conjunction." Brockman was an unlettered German farmer, and all this astrological stuff meant little to him, but he was determined that the marriage should take place on whatever date Kate regarded as propitious. It appears that Brockman did not know the Benders had fled until several days after the fact, but as soon as he heard about it he began asking questions of everybody in the neighborhood.

Because of this the mob learned of his association with the Benders. When they went to see him, it was obvious that he was much upset—and no wonder, since he had just seen 11 corpses dug up in his darling's backyard!

Rudolph Brockman answered all questions frankly enough. He said that he was in love with Kate Bender, and had certainly intended to marry her, but that he had not the least suspicion that the Benders were a gang of murderers. He said that Kate had intimated to him that old man Bender, in his younger days, had killed a man back in Pennsylvania: because of this the Benders had fled to Michigan and later to the Kansas prairies. But all this happened long ago, and the whole Bender tribe seemed to him honest people, trying to make an honest living. He said he had overheard some of the conversations in German which the Benders carried on in the presence of their guests, but it was merely "blackguard talk," and that there had never been any mention of robbery or murder.

Some members of the posse searched Brockman, and found a gold ring inscribed "To Kate," and a tintype picture of Kate in a little black frame with gold edges. They also found some love-letters from Kate, but these were written mostly in German. Brockman refused to translate the letters, but a German named Biedewolf looked them over despite Brockman's protests, and laughed at what he called their "foolishness." But he testified that there was nothing about murder or robbery in the letters. Without any good reason, it appears, the mob decided to hang Brockman, although several prominent citizens protested against this action. They did hang poor Brockman, and rode away leaving him suspended from a tree, but some friends cut him down immediately and he was revived.

Years later some descendants of Brockman, who were still living in Cherryvale, denied the whole story. There is some evidence that Brockman was friendly with Kate Bender, and that he was roughly treated by a mob shortly after the bodies were unearthed at Benders' Tavern, but it is probably true that he knew nothing of the criminal activities of the Bender family. The fact that Brockman was never prosecuted as an accessory to the murders seems to indicate that there was no evidence against him that would stand up in court.

There have been plenty of crimes in southeastern Kansas, both before and after the Benders' day, but no other bloody affair has so infuriated the easy-going populace. "Probably the greatest number of men under arms in Kansas since the Civil War took part in the search for the fleeing family," said a Kansas newspaper. Governor Thomas Osborn's office issued "Dead or Alive" posters, which were stuck up all over Kansas and sent to peace officers in many parts of the United States, particularly in the West and Southwest. These posters carried careful descriptions of each member of the family. I have been unable to obtain a copy of Governor Osborn's handbill, but old-timers have told me that the state offered a reward of $1,000 for each of the Benders—$4,000 altogether, **dead or alive.**

For weeks and even months after the bodies were found, people came from the North and East, looking for their relatives who had come to Kansas and had never been heard from again. A number of mistaken identifications were made, as is usual in such cases. One woman, after having identified one of the bodies as that of her missing husband, was thunderstruck a few days later to find him alive and well, running a saloon at Pittsburg, Kansas.

"It was a strange thing," said one old resident, "to see people fightin' over them old mouldy corpses like they was made of gold! I seen one of 'em identified four times, eash time under a different name. And us neighbors all knowed who it was, all the time! But we never let on—just let the damn fools have their fun." In some cases strangers probably claimed the better-dressed bodies, hoping to profit in case the Benders were captured and the stolen money recovered. In time all of the 11 corpses were identified except two. And as late as 1910 there were still people in Kansas who claimed to have recognized even these.

All through the Summer of 1873 little bands of armed men rode snarling through southeast Kansas. Several of them ventured over into Missouri, and down across the border of the Indian Territory. Some of these raiders had no legal authority at all, but they did not hesitate to arrest people, and question them, and search their homes. Rudolph Brockman was not the only man who was tortured by a mob trying to elicit information about the Bender murders. The Kansas pioneers were not men to submit tamely to such treatment, and many bloody fights were reported. One small-town editor said that more men were killed by the posses who were searching for the Benders, than had ever been murdered in the Bender Tavern. But this was doubtless an exaggeration.

Somewhere west of Independence a posse came upon a group of Gypsies camping by the roadside. At the pistol's point they forced these people to bring every movable object out of their vans and spread them out in the dusty road, while the officers—one of them did have a deputy sheriff's commission—examined every bit of this stuff to see if it could be related somehow to the Bender crimes. Finding nothing incriminating, they made the whole tribe of men, women and children strip to the skin, and stand there in the road while the deputy examined their clothing. The poor Gypsies declared two days later that they had never heard of the Benders, and even then had no idea what crime had been committed.

Another group of "Bender detectives" located some Negro squatters down on the Territory line, south of the present town of Coffeyville, Kansas. In searching one of the Negro huts, these ruffians found some cheap jewelry which they imagined was somehow derived from the Bender victims. The leader of this gang began cuffing some Negro women around, and firing his pistol at a Negro man's feet, in order to make them tell where they had obtained the jewelry. It developed later that the stuff had been stolen, in the burglary of a little store, but it had nothing to do with the Benders. Armed Negroes from other cabins in the neighborhood began crawling up through the brush and there would have been a regular race riot, with blood spilled on both sides, if some sensible white men had not happened along and forced the posse to decamp.

These amateur sheriffs and sleuths and marshals lost interest after a few weeks of hell-raising, and the Bender hunt was abandoned by all save a few enthusiasts. There were two generally recognized reasons for the Benders' successful escape—they had at least a week's start on their pursuers, and they carried plenty of cash. The officers estimated from the amount of money that the Benders were said to have obtained, that the four fugitives had about $50,000 among them—a sum equal to perhaps $200,000 at the present time. Nearly all of the regularly elected peace officers believed that the Benders had fled south to the Indian Territory, and perhaps continued on into Texas. The amateur sleuths, many of whom came from New York, inclined to the view that the Benders would return to their old haunts in Michigan or Pennsylvania, since it was believed that they had lived in both of these places.

When Colonel York had been convinced that neither the regular officers nor the amateurs were going to catch the Benders, he started out himself with a small posse and followed the murderers' trail from Thayer, Kansas, where the team was found, down through the Territory into Texas. Here they mingled with gamblers and horse-thieves and all kinds of frontier riff-raff, always hoping to hear a word about the Benders. There were two men in this posse who knew all four of the Benders by sight, and they rode hundreds of miles to have a look at suspects located here and there, but always with negative results. Some newspaper writers have denied that Colonel York himself ever led a posse, but there is good reason to believe that he did. He was absent from Fort Scott for several months in 1873, and it is my opinion that the men who claimed to have accompanied him to the Indian Territory and Texas were telling the truth.

The general opinion that the Benders escaped is well stated in the reminiscences of L. F. Dick, who had lived near Cherryvale and was acquainted with the Bender family. Dick always claimed that the Benders abandoned the team at Thayer, Kansas and boarded a southbound train. He believed that young Johnny Bender and Kate went to Denison, Texas, where Johnny worked on a railroad construction gang, and Kate operated a grease-joint for section-hands. To the objection that the Benders had so much money that they surely would not work under these conditions, it was pointed out that the Benders had plenty of money in Kansas, but they were not above any sort of labor which masked their real source of income. Old man Bender and his wife had gone to St. Louis, according to Dick's theory, but after a few months they also moved to Denison, although they now claimed that they were not related to Kate and Johnny at all.

When Colonel York heard a report of the Benders' presence in Denison he had just returned from his own long pursuit of them in the Territory. He was tired of the whole business, and evidently convinced that the Benders were gone beyond recovery. So he did not go to Denison himself, but called in C. J. Peckham, Henry Beers and Jim Snoddy. These men were willing to make another effort to run the Benders to earth for the rewards which were still in force, providing that Colonel York would pay their expenses. York said he was willing to to do this, and handed over $1,000 in advance. "They followed the Benders to Denison and from there to within 50 miles of El Paso," runs Dick's account of the chase, "and there they lost the trail. Later they found it again and followed it for 200 miles, into a community where the people would not allow the officers to remove any person there. The state of Texas refused to assist and the government refused to send its soldiers into the community to make arrests," so Peckham and his men came back to Kansas empty-handed...

The attitude of the Texas authorities seems strange to us now, but things were different in the 70's, and Dick's account of the Peckham party's rebuff might be near the truth. The Texans had little confidence in the United States troops stationed in Texas, but preferred to depend upon a kind of state police called the Texas Rangers. The Rangers were nearly all ex-Confederates. They were engaged in fighting Indians and Mexican outlaws on their frontiers, besides battling at home with some of the toughest bandits and ruffians who ever terrorized the West. The Lone Star state had been harrased and looted by carpet-baggers for nearly a decade, and Northern officers were naturally unpopular in Texas. So the Peckham possemen were told that they could go to hell, or back to Kansas. After all, these Benders were not accused of anything worse than killin' a few Yankees!

According to Dick's story, Kate and Johnny realized that they were lucky, and stayed on in Texas and New Mexico. But in the Fall of 1874 old man Bender and his wife went back to Michigan, where they lived quietly for about five years. Dick says flatly that old man Bender killed himself in 1879, but I have never been able to find out anything definite about this alleged suicide. But at some time between 1879 and 1889 it appears that many people believed that both Kate and Mrs. Bender were living in Michigan.

In 1889 two women who gave their names as Mrs. Frances E. McCann and Mrs. L. Davis were arrested at Berrian, Michigan, and brought back to Oswego, Kansas. Several old-timers went to see them in the jail at Oswego, and positively identified them as old Mrs. Bender and her daughter Kate. The women from Michigan denied everything, but were afraid they might be lynched by the savage Kansans before they could establish their identity. The following story is from the Kansas City *Journal*, dated November 20, 1889: "After the examination of 16 witnesses, seven of whom declare that the prisoners are the Benders and seven of whom say they are not, and two not having any opinion, the justice of the peace decided that there is probable cause for holding them without bail for trial in the district court."

The same newspaper says of the trial, which was held a week later, that "the courtroom has been packed with citizens for two days, and never was such interest manifested in a trial in Labette county. One witness for the state and six for the defense were on the stand today, besides the prisoners themselves who took the stand in their own defense. Mrs. Frances E. McCann and Mrs. L. Davis are the defendants. Judge Webb and Mr. James, the attorneys for the defense, laugh at the idea of their clients ever being convicted, while the great crowd of people seems equally divided in opinion. The prisoners now accept the situation, and seem not to be affected." After hours of wrangling, the attorneys for the defense convinced the court that a mistake had been made, and that the women were not Mrs. John Bender and Kate Bender. When Mrs. McCann and Mrs. Davis were released, they left Oswego at once. Notwithstanding the decision of the court, many of the old settlers believed that the women *were* the Benders, and their lawyers told them their lives were in danger if they remained in Labette county over night.

According to the official records, the Benders had escaped all the posses sent after them, and were still listed as fugitives from justice. It is certainly true that nobody ever publicly admitted that he had killed or captured any of the Benders, and no formal claim was ever made for the rewards offered by the state of Kansas and the relatives of the victims.

Nevertheless, many people in Kansas were firmly convinced that all four of the Benders were dead. An old gentleman in Girard, Kansas, once told me that two men who sat in the courtroom at Oswego, during the investigation of Mrs. McCann and Mrs. Davis, *knew* that both women were innocent. These two men, according to my informant, had been present when Mrs. John Bender and Kate Bender were shot to death. One of the men had fired four shots from his own revolver into Kate's body, and members of his family prized this pistol for many years as the weapon which killed the Kansas murderess. According to this version of the tale, the posse overtook the Benders near what is now the Oklahoma-Kansas line. The four killers jumped out of their buggy and fled into a cornfield, firing as they ran. The pursuers did their best to capture some of them alive, but old man Bender and Johnny were killed early in the fight. Mrs. Bender was captured, but as the officers approached she fired a pocket-pistol at them, and was immediately shot to death. Kate Bender came near escaping, but one of her pursuers pushed on ahead of his fellows, and finally saw her hiding behind a shock of corn. As he came up she fired with an Army Colts, and gave him a painful wound in the right leg. He returned the fire with his own revolver, and Kate fell to the ground. She was still alive, however, but in a cold fury he limped forward and fired three more shots as she rolled about beside the corn-shock. Another man came running up, and fired several more shots into the body, which now lay still.

If we are to accept this variant of the tale, the members of the posse collected the four bodies, and were about to load them into the wagon, intending to take them back to Cherryvale and collect the rewards, which were said to total about $5,000. When they searched the Benders, however, they found a large sum of money—some say that it amounted to more than $40,000. So they sat down and talked a while, discussing what was to be done with the money. Finally they decided that it would be best for them to divide the loot among themselves—since there were only seven men in this posse. After they had divided the money, and also a hatful of gold watches and diamond rings, they buried the Benders where they fell and drove up to the camp later known as South Coffeyville, where they went on a big drunk that lasted several days. After a week or so of recuperation, they returned soberly to their homes, with most of the money on their persons, in fine leather money-belts which they had taken from the bodies of the Benders. When they got back to Kansas they reported that they had found no trace of the Bender family, and had decided to give up the quest and return to their farming.

Whether or not this story is true I have no way of knowing, at this late date. Edmund Pearson, who wrote histories of many great crimes in his day, collected a lot of material on the Bender case, and he appeared to favor this theory. I know, as Mr. Pearson probably did not, that there were families in Labette and Crawford counties only a few short years ago, who claimed to have positive knowledge that the Benders were all killed as described in the preceding paragraphs. Some of my own relatives have told me of seeing old guns, watches and money-belts in the possession of pioneer families in Kansas, who told them in confidence that these objects were relics of the bloody Benders.

The persistence of this version of the Bender legend is surprising. Whenever the Bender story is retold in a crime magazine, or a newspaper, or even mentioned on the radio, the tale of their killing by a small posse in a cornfield pops up in letters to the editor. Several years ago a number of photographs connected with the Bender tragedy appeared in *PIC* magazine, and on March 19, 1940, the editor published a letter from Louis S. Ross, Lansing, Michigan, which I quote in part: "It might interest you to know that during the time of the Kate Bender reign of terror, my grandfather, Mr. Shedrick Ross, drove a stagecoach between Coffeyville and Independence, Kansas. He related to my father that he had visited the Bender Inn on several occasions. He was also with the posse that killed Kate Bender. He told my father that Kate Bender was found hiding in a cornfield, at which place she met her death. She was shot to death by the posse. She was hiding in a cornshock when the posse found her. They opened fire on her. The cornshock was shattered to ribbons, and Kate Bender was dead with 24 bullet holes in her body."

The reader will note that Mr. Ross offers no explanation of why the posse did not report the killing to the authorities in Kansas, or why they did not claim the reward. And the letter written by Mr. Ross is only one of many such communications, scores of which have found their way into print. If Kate Bender was really killed by a posse, as so many people have said, I can see only one reason why the fact was so carefully concealed over such a long period. And that reason is that Kate was carrying a large sum of money, so that it was more profitable for the killers to suppress the facts and keep the money, than to reveal the killing and collect the rewards that were offered for the Benders, "dead or alive."

And yet—one wonders. Why did not the members of the posse divide the cash found on the Benders, and then bring the bodies in and claim the rewards too? If any questions were asked, they had only to say that no money was found on the bodies, except a few dollars in the men's pockets.

Another school of thought in the matter of the Bender mystery holds that the wagon left near Thayer was only a blind. According to this theory, the Benders proceded in another wagon to Chanute, Kansas, where they made contact with some of the Gypsy or Indian outlaws with which they were connected in the popular mind. Telling these confederates that the team and wagon were stolen and must therefore be kept out of sight, the four Benders' went down to the railroad station and bought tickets for some unnamed town in Texas. They got off the train at Chetopa, Kansas, where they stole four horses and rode south for a while. Then they turned the horses loose, hid the saddles and bridles, and started through the Indian Territory on foot. According to this tale the Benders were captured, not by any of the regular posses, but by a small party financed by the relatives of a man who was murdered by the Benders. Before being captured, the Benders had secreted their money in a brush-pile, but this strategem availed them nothing. The savage captors, driven by motives of both greed and revenge, resolved to torture the prisoners until they told where the cash was hidden. They knocked the old man and Johnny about for a while, but got no information out of them. Then one of the ruffians cut a stout hickory switch, and applied it to Kate's bare back and legs until she finally broke down and revealed the whereabouts of the money, though the other three Benders cursed her roundly for "turning traitor." In possession of the sack of money, one of the party felt so jovial that he was all set for setting the Benders at liberty, but was voted down by the others. The drunken argument lasted all night, and finally ended in a fight. One man was shot to death, and another cut so severely that he died a few hours later. The surviving members of the party hanged all four of the Benders in a little grove of blackjack trees, and rode on about their business. Three days later two of these men returned with picks and buried the six corpses in a single grave.

The men in this lynching party, according to the old story, were not deeply rooted in Kansas, and only one of them ever returned to that state. This man, it is said, became a coal-miner and was killed in a mine explosion near Frontenac, Kansas, in the 90's. The other members of this party rambled on down into the Territory, where they all ended badly in true story-book fashion. The ruffian who had flogged Kate became a genuine desperado, and his name was associated with that of another strange frontier character known to history only as Blue Duck. And even Blue Duck is remembered now as one of the many lovers of Belle Starr, the so-called "Queen of the Bandits," who terrorized the Territory in the 1880's.

There are other theories to account for the Benders' disappearance, of course, and some of them were developed at considerable length in penny-dreadful magazines, published in Philadelphia and New York. There were several paper-backed books purporting to give all the mysterious inside information about the Bender affair, sold by newsagents on trains all over the country. It has been said that garbled accounts of the Benders' career were published in Great Britain, and even translated into several foreign languages, but I have not seen any of these translations. I believe that most of the persons who were in Kansas at the time, and who might conceivably have obtained information not given to the press and the writers of the magazine thrillers, inclined to the view that the Benders were killed in 1873.

As in all such cases, there are many people who believe that the criminals got off scot-free, and that the younger Benders were living only a few years ago. J. T. James, who wrote a book about the Bender case, believed that all four of the Benders journeyed by rail to Vinita, in the Indian Territory, and then proceeded on horseback to Denison, Texas. Some of Mr. James' disciples believe that the Benders were captured by a small posse, and that Kate purchased their freedom for $20,000 on the barrel-head. There used to be a United States Deputy Marshal in Oklahoma who claimed to know something about this; he once remarked that he had written a full account of the matter to be sent to the Historical Society after his death. This man died several years ago, but his relatives say that no such account was found among his papers.

In many of these tales about the Benders' alleged escape, and about their life therafter, we find certain flat statements with no evidence whatever to support them. One of these assertions is that old man Bender committed suicide in Michigan, late in 1789. Mrs. Bender is supposed to have died in Texas, in 1882 or 1883. Another story is that Kate married a United States Deputy Marshal, one of the men who had pursued her family at the time of the exodus from Kansas. About the turn of the century people were always claiming to have met Kate Bender in the street somewhere—in New Orleans, in Mexico City, in New York, in Havana, and once even in Paris. She was always described as a distinguished woman, slender and quietly dressed. As late as 1910, some of Kate's old acquaintances got the idea that she was living on 12th Street, in Kansas City. They even wrote to the newspapers about it. And in 1938 a well-known weekly magazine stated, as if it were a historical fact, that Johnny Bender died in Amarillo, Texas, in 1925.

Only a short time ago, in a syndicated column, there appeared the following: "Is Kate Bender, the most blood-thirsty and diabolic minded woman the New World has ever produced, still living? This is a question that has come to the minds of thousands of persons who remember her horrible history. Is the arch murderess of Kansas still alive?"

Well, I believe I can answer the columnist's question, without recourse to astrology or crystal-gazing or even tea-leaves. A little elementary arithmetic is good enough for me. Our best witnesses agree that Kate was about 20 years old when she came to Kansas in 1870. If she is alive now she must be 94, and women of Kate's type seldom reach that age. I think we may safely assume that the arch murderess is dead, and has been dead for a long time. But if by any chance I am wrong about this, and Kate Bender is still breathing as I write these words, there is still no cause for panic on the banks of the Verdigris. Women 94 years old do not go about bashing skulls and slitting throats, even in the rarefield air of windy Kansas.

CPSIA information can be obtained
at www.ICGtesting.com
Printed in the USA
BVHW041753210421
605537BV00011B/1053